Deinonychus

Written by Rupert Oliver
Illustrated by Roger Payne

© 1984 Rourke Enterprises, Inc.

Copyright © 1984 Martspress Ltd., Nork Way
Banstead, Surrey, SM7 1PB.

Library of Congress Cataloging in Publication Data

Oliver, Rupert.
  Deinonychus.

  Summary: Describes the physical characteristics,
habits, and natural environment of the dinosaur known
as Deinonychus.
  1. Deinonychus—Juvenile literature.   [1. Deinonychus.
2. Dinosaurs]   I. Payne, Roger, fl. 1969-   ill.
II. Title.
QE862.S3O45   1984   567.9'7   84-17791
ISBN 0-86592-213-6

Rourke Enterprises, Inc.
Vero Beach, FL 32964

Rhamphorhynchus

Pteranodon

Pterodactyl

Ankylosaurus

Dimetrodon

Iguanodon

Tricondon

Deinonychus

Archaeopteryx

Ichthyosaurus

Plesiosaurus

Deinonychus

Nothosaurus

Deinonychus shifted his position to make himself more comfortable. A sharp twig had been digging into his ribs. He had been resting in the shade of the tree for several hours now.

Idly, he raised his great claw and scratched himself behind the ear. The terrible heat of the noon sun was too strong for Deinonychus, but it was beginning to cool down now. His ear still itched. Deinonychus lifted his foot up again and scratched himself more vigorously. This time he disturbed a large insect which flew away. It had been biting him and sucking his blood. Deinonychus was comfortable now and he dozed off again. As he dozed a butterfly flew past on its colorful wings. Deinonychus did not like the hot weather but it suited the insects.

It was late in the afternoon and the sun was not so hot when Deinonychus woke. The insects still buzzed around Deinonychus, but he did not itch. Slowly he rose to his feet. He felt fresh and fit. Deinonychus yawned and licked his lips. He felt thirsty. The heat of the day had dried him out, even though he had rested in the shade. Deinonychus set off to walk to the river.

Following a well used track between the trees and bushes, Deinonychus reached the water's edge. The river was full of fresh, cool water. The arrival of Deinonychus disturbed a pair of turtles who splashed back into the safety of the river.

Deinonychus walked out across the mud flats to the water. He bent down to drink. Suddenly, the whole water surface seemed to explode with spray and foam right at the feet of Deinonychus. In sudden fear, Deinonychus stepped back as a vicious pair of jaws snapped shut, inches from his leg. Out of the flying water emerged the head and body of a crocodile. It had been lying in shallow water waiting. Deinonychus had walked right into the trap.

Quickly, Deinonychus scrambled back across the mud to the dry land. The crocodile did not follow Deinonychus. It preferred to sink back into the water and wait for another animal to come to drink.

Deinonychus ran into the trees lining the river. He had not completely satisfied his thirst, but he did not want to go back to the river if the crocodile was still there. Perhaps if he went to another part of the river there would be no crocodiles.

Suddenly Deinonychus heard a distant crash. He stood still. Then another crash sounded out, much nearer. Now Deinonychus could hear heavy footsteps and the sound of smashing branches. Something was coming and whatever it was, it was very large. Deinonychus was worried, that it was a meat eater. It would be safest to hide.

Deinonychus pushed his way into a thick bush and waited. The sound of footsteps came closer and closer and then Deinonychus could see a looming bulk as the creature came into sight. Deinonychus need not have worried. The newcomer was a Tenontosaurus. This dinosaur was big, but it ate plants and was no danger to Deinonychus.

When it had gone Deinonychus came out of hiding and looked around. The Tenontosaurus had left a path of flattened and broken vegetation behind it as it smashed a way through the forest. Deinonychus decided to follow the path. It would be easier than picking his own route.

Deinonychus walked along the tracks of the Tenontosaurus until he reached the edge of the forest. Instead of finding himself at a river, Deinonychus was at the edge of a wide plain. He could see for miles across the landscape. On the plain was a group of animals. When Deinonychus saw what they were he felt his stomach rumbling. They were Psittacosaurs. Deinonychus suddenly felt very hungry.

Deinonychus knew that he would have to be very careful when hunting the Psittacosaurs. If they saw him they would run away and Deinonychus would have to go hungry.

Deinonychus walked out on to the plain as if he had not seen the Psittacosaurs. He did not walk straight toward them. He walked toward a small clump of trees to one side. One Psittacosaurus looked up from its feeding to watch the Deinonychus. When it saw that the Deinonychus was not coming toward it, the Psittacosaurus continued eating.

Using the trees as cover, Deinonychus was able to get close to the Psittacosaurs without being seen. As soon as he left the trees and moved toward the plant eaters he was seen. One of the Psittacosaurs gave a bellow of alarm and started to run. The other Psittacosaurs heard the cry and also began to run. If he was to stand any chance of a meal, Deinonychus too, had to run. The chase had begun.

Using his long legs Deinonychus bounded after the retreating Psittacosaurs. One of the plant eaters was slower than the others. Perhaps he was old or ill, either way he would be the easiest to catch. Deinonychus decided to chase him. Across the plain the two dinosaurs raced. Their feet kicked up the dust as they ran.

Deinonychus was gaining on the Psittacosaurus. Then it stumbled. Now it stood no chance against Deinonychus. Deinonychus leapt high into the air. He brought his hind legs up under his body and raised his great claws. He had judged the leap perfectly. Deinonychus landed right on top of the Psittacosaurus. His huge, sickle-shaped claws ripped deep into the plant eater. The Psittacosaurus gave a roar of pain and tried to escape, but Deinonychus was hungry and plunged his terrible claws into the soft body of the Psittacosaurus again and again. Within seconds it was all over and the Psittacosaurus lay dead at the feet of Deinonychus.

Deinonychus climbed off the still body of the Psittacosaurus. The long chase had made him breathless. Then he began to eat. He bent down and tore great mouthfuls of meat from the carcass.

As Deinonychus began to eat he saw a pair of small Coelurosaurs standing nearby. Deinonychus roared at them angrily, but they did not move away. Deinonychus continued eating. While he was still eating, one of the Coelurosaurs dashed in and grabbed a mouthful of meat. Deinonychus left the body of the Psittacosaurus when he was full. Then both the Coelurosaurs dashed in and began to eat.

As Deinonychus moved away the sun was setting. He felt much better with a full stomach and moved off to find somewhere to rest for the night. Behind him the small animals continued to squabble over pieces of meat, but the sounds of their fight faded as Deinonychus moved away. In the shelter of some bushes Deinonychus found a soft patch of ferns to lie on. He settled down and closed his eyes. It had been a tiring day and Deinonychus was very tired. Soon he was fast asleep.

Deinonychus and Early Cretaceous North America

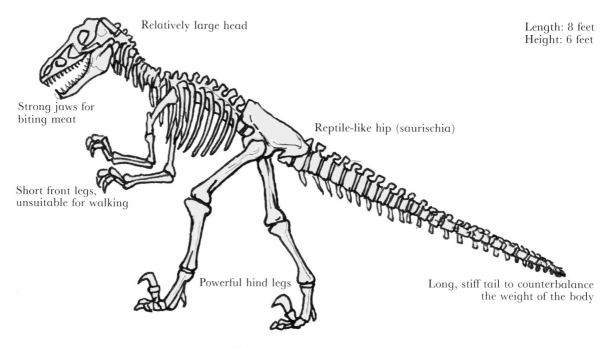

Relatively large head

Length: 8 feet
Height: 6 feet

Strong jaws for biting meat

Reptile-like hip (saurischia)

Short front legs, unsuitable for walking

Powerful hind legs

Long, stiff tail to counterbalance the weight of the body

Skeleton of Deinonychus

When did Deinonychus live?
The Age of the Dinosaurs began about 225 million years ago and lasted for some 180 million years. Scientists have divided this era, which has been called the Mesozoic, into three periods. The first was the Triassic, the second the Jurassic and the third the Cretaceous. Deinonychus lived during the early part of the Cretaceous. It lived about 125 million years ago.

Where did Deinonychus live?
The fossils of Deinonychus have been found in Montana in the United States but Montana was a very different place 125 million years ago. There were no Rocky Mountains. The earth movements that were to result in the Rockies had not even begun. The landscape was very much like that in the book and would only become mountainous towards the end of the Cretaceous.

It is also interesting to note that western North America was not linked to the eastern part of the continent. It is thought that a shallow sea ran from Canada down to the Gulf of Mexico. Instead, scientists believe, the western part of the continent was linked with Asia. The fact that dinosaurs, similar to Deinonychus have been found in Asia but not in eastern America, seems to support this idea. Indeed, deinonychosaurs may have first evolved in eastern Asia.

The Terrible Claw
Deinonychus means 'terrible claw' and it is easy to see why scientists gave it this name. The second toe on each hind foot ended in a 5 inch long claw. There can be little doubt that this was its main killing weapon. Deinonychus could also run very fast. When it saw a likely victim its speed would enable it to run the victim down. When Deinonychus had reached its prey it would leap upon it and kick and slash at it with its claw, just as some birds do.

Some scientists think that Deinonychus may have hidden in ambush for its prey, alternatively it may have hunted in packs as lions do today. It certainly had a larger brain than other dinosaurs and may have been intelligent enough to hunt in groups.

Deinonychus Ancestors
Deinonychus was a meat-eating dinosaur of the Saurischian, (lizard-hipped) group. All the meat-eating and some plant-eating dinosaurs belonged to this group. All plant-eating dinosaurs belonged to the Ornithischian, (bird-hipped) group.

Deinonychus clearly represented a distinct form of meat-eating dinosaur. Scientists have therefore placed it and a few similar dinosaurs, in a special family known as deinonychosaurs. It is thought that this family was an offshoot of the highly successful coelurosaur family which survived throughout the entire Age of Dinosaurs. The fast-running and agile deinonychosaurs were certainly very different from the larger and more ponderous carnosaurs such as Tyrannosaurus Rex. They were much more like the small coelurosaurs which could scamper around in the undergrowth. It is thought that one type of coelurosaur changed into the deinonychosaurs at the start of the Cretaceous period, about 135 million years ago. Phaedrolosaurus, a dinosaur from China, may have been one of these ancestral deinonychosaurs.

A Time of Change
Deinonychus lived during the early part of the Cretaceous period, a time of great change for the dinosaurs. Throughout the previous ninety million years the Saurischian dinosaurs had ruled the world. The future belonged to the Ornithischians.

During the long Jurassic period the most important type of plant-eater had been the Sauropods. Sauropods were giant Saurischian dinosaurs with long tails and long necks. Brontosaurus was a kind of Sauropod. Sauropods can be seen on page 12. By the time Deinonychus hunted in North America Sauropods were becoming rarer. Their place was being taken by many new kinds of Ornithischians. Tenontosaurus, which can be seen on page 10, was one of these. It belonged to the iguanodontid family of dinosaurs. This family included the famous Iguanodon from Europe which was related to the highly successful duckbilled dinosaurs. Psittacosaurus was also an Ornithischian dinosaur. It was probably the ancestor of the ceratopsian dinosaurs, a group which included the mighty Triceratops.

Other animals were changing as well. The flying reptiles were changing from the long-tailed forms, such as Rhamphorhynchus, to the short-tailed Pterosaurs. Birds had evolved from reptile ancestors and were developing into a wide range of species.

The early Cretaceous period was an important time for life on earth.

The Deinonychus with (inset) the large sickle-shaped claw on its hind leg with which attacked its prey.